FOR YOUR HOME

NATURAL COLOR PALETTES

FOR YOUR HOME

NATURAL COLOR PALETTES

Ellen M. Plante

FRIEDMAN/FAIRFAX
PUBLISHERS

Dedication

For those who contemplate the beauty that surrounds us, especially color.

Acknowledgments

Special thanks to Hallie Einhorn, my editor at the Michael Friedman Publishing Group.

A FRIEDMAN/FAIRFAX BOOK

©2000 by Michael Friedman Publishing Group, Inc.

Library of Congress Cataloging-in-Publication Data

Plante, Ellen M.
    Natural color palettes / by Ellen M. Plante.
       p. cm. — (For your home)
    Includes index.
    ISBN 1-56799-918-2
    1. Color in interior decoration. 2. Nature (Aesthetics) I. Title. II. Series.

NK2115.5.C6 P535 2000
747'.94—dc21
                                            99-049515

Editor: Hallie Einhorn
Art Director: Jeff Batzli
Designer: Charles Donahue
Photography Editor: Erin Feller
Production: Camille Lee and Leslie Wong

Color separations by Fine Arts Repro House Co., Ltd.
Printed in Hong Kong by Midas Printing Limited

1 3 5 7 9 10 8 6 4 2

For bulk purchases and special sales, please contact:
Friedman/Fairfax Publishers
Attention: Sales Department
15 West 26th Street
New York, New York 10010
212/685-6610 FAX 212/685-1307

Visit our website:
www.metrobooks.com

Contents

INTRODUCTION

IN ALL THINGS OF NATURE THERE IS SOMETHING OF THE MARVELOUS.

—Aristotle (384–322 B.C.E.)

Marvelous indeed—especially when it comes to color. Consider for just a moment how the words "natural color palette" immediately bring to mind the great outdoors. Standing in a field of wildflowers, we are mesmerized by the combination of both vibrant and soft hues. Gazing at a winter landscape, we're overcome by the spirit of beauty played out in subtle whites and grays. Or, strolling on an autumn day, we can be riveted by the display of leaves changing from green to russet and gold.

Take a good look around you. Notice the peaceful blue of a cloudless sky or the more intense color of a churning sea. Pay attention to how light seems to alter natural colors as the hours of the day go by—white clouds can turn to pink, deep red, or lavender during a sunset. It's no wonder we long to bring such colors inside and surround ourselves with a palette that evokes tranquility and a sense of well-being.

Natural colors, inspired by nature and created using natural elements, have a long history of use in interior design. Early homes had rugged walls constructed of logs, stone, or clay. Bricks and tiles were later used for functional as well as decorative purposes. These earthy substances were joined by other natural materials, such as linen, cotton, silk, and muslin, that were used on furnishings and for window dressings. Colorful decorative accents, reminiscent of the select shades found in nature, were created with natural dyes and minerals to add a cheerful note to both rural and urban homes.

Opposite: IN THIS ELEGANT LIVING ROOM, WALLPAPER SPORTING STRIPES OF TAUPE AND WHITE PLAYS HOST TO UPHOLSTERED PIECES BEARING SIMILAR HUES. A LOVELY BROWN AREA RUG, BEARING SWIRLS OF SANDY BEIGE, SITS ATOP NATURAL FIBER MATTING TO DEFINE THE CONVERSATION AREA. OTHER ELEMENTS THAT PAY HOMAGE TO NATURE COME INTO PLAY, INCLUDING NUMEROUS LEAFY PATTERNS AND TWO DECORATIVE TABLE LAMPS (ONE SPORTING A PAINTED PALM TREE, THE OTHER SPROUTING GILDED LEAVES). AS A RESULT, THE ROOM VIVIDLY RECALLS THE OUTDOORS WHILE PROVIDING ALL THE CREATURE COMFORTS OF HOME.

Above: OFF-WHITE WALLS AND COORDINATING WINDOW SHADES FASHION A DISTRACTION-FREE BACKDROP IN THIS CONTEMPORARY WORK SPACE. THE NON-FUSSY WINDOW TREATMENT AND THE PALE, SMOOTH SURFACES OF THE MODERN DESK AND BENCH NOT ONLY BLEND EFFORTLESSLY TO ESTABLISH A NEUTRAL COLOR SCHEME, BUT ALSO WORK TOGETHER TO GIVE THE AREA A SLEEK LOOK.

During the eighteenth century, interiors often bore neutral color schemes, with gray, buff, and various shades of white being the simplest hues to create. Terra-cotta and umber were made from clay, while certain vegetables and flowers were called upon to make dyes that would transform homespun fabrics into a kaleidoscope of deep or softly faded hues. For example, cranberries were used to turn fabric red, while ragweed flowers or iris petals were employed to concoct a lovely shade of green. Minerals, too, were an important ingredient in early dyes—blue was derived from lapis lazuli and green from malachite.

By the late nineteenth century, synthetic dyes had been developed, thereby expanding the color choices available for home decor. The Victorians made wonderful use of color in their eclectic, sometimes shocking interiors. With the exception of the Arts and Crafts Movement (which called for the use of natural dyes in printed fabric), interior design progressed steadily into the twentieth century with a bright new focus on the development of color, courtesy of advances in technology that presented new possibilities for decorating the home.

Trends and styles may come and go, but one constant seems to be a deeply rooted desire for peaceful retreats from the outside world. Today, this still translates into rooms that echo the beauty of nature.

How, then, do you go about selecting a natural color palette for your own home? Colors you find yourself drawn to again and again often form a basis from which to start. Blue is regarded as an all-time favorite, with green usually running a close second. No matter what your preference, the almost limitless variations available can seem overwhelming. However, they can be narrowed down by keeping some key points in mind.

When it comes to "talking the talk," most colors are considered to be either "warm" or "cool" and are linked to certain emotions or moods. Warm colors include vibrant reds, oranges, and yellows, as well as such lighter tints as pink and apricot. Since warm colors are energizing and stimulating, they often prove ideal in rooms with limited natural lighting. This sensation of vitality also makes these colors appropriate for high-activity rooms: picture a yellow kitchen or a deep red dining room. And let's not forget the home office, where a warm color can help increase productivity.

In contrast, cool colors, such as blues and greens, are calming, infusing the rooms they adorn with serenity. These hues are shown off to their best advantage in areas with an abundance of natural light. When selecting a natural palette for a small room, keep in mind that cool colors will make the space appear larger. These relaxing hues are often favored for the bedroom (where quiet repose is ideal), library, and bath, the latter being increasingly viewed as a pleasure/relaxation room more than a strictly utilitarian space.

Choosing a natural color palette for any given room may be as simple as building around a favorite rug, a

Above: WE USUALLY THINK OF BEDROOMS IN TERMS OF COOL COLORS, BUT WARM HUES CAN BE TONED DOWN TO CREATE A SOOTHING PALETTE. HERE, A SPECIAL PAINTING TECHNIQUE GIVES THE OCHER WALLS AND CEILING A FADED LOOK THAT CREATES A RELAXING AMBIENCE. POPPY-COLORED BEDDING RAISES THE TEMPERATURE SLIGHTLY, BUT THIS EFFECT IS TEMPERED BY THE LOW-KEY DEMEANOR OF THE PAINT-CHIPPED WROUGHT-IRON BED FRAME.

Above: SINCE THIS TRADITIONAL DINING ROOM HAS A PRIMARILY NEUTRAL BACKDROP, THE DARK GREEN PLATES DISPLAYED ON THE HUTCH REALLY STAND OUT AND SERVE AS THE SPACE'S FOCAL POINT. MORE SUBTLE TOUCHES OF GREEN APPEAR IN THE CANDLES, AREA RUG, AND STENCILED BORDERS RUNNING ALONGSIDE THE CHAIR RAIL AND CORNICE. OFTENTIMES, THE RESTRAINED USE OF A DEEP SHADE CREATES THE PERFECT MEASURE OF VISUAL IMPACT.

treasured painting, or a piece of furniture. Inspiration may come from the view outside your window or the longing to re-create the ambience of a woodland cottage or a seaside retreat. No matter where the idea originates, selecting specific colors will be easier if you know the difference between a "shade" and a "tint," and understand the concept of "tone." A shade is developed by adding black to a specific color, while a tint is the end result after adding white. We often refer to pastels as tints and muted colors as shades. Tone simply refers to the depth of color (how light or dark) and applies to both tints and shades.

Regardless of your decorative style, almost any natural palette can be incorporated. Remember that walls are not the only elements to consider when establishing the color scheme. The beauty of the outdoors can be reflected in flooring, the ceiling, window dressings, furnishings, and decorative accessories. Upholstery, carpeting, drapes, and treasured objects all come into play. As with any chosen palette, natural colors can be used to define different spaces or to cause one room to flow smoothly into another. Color is also an excellent means of drawing attention to architectural embellishments, such as moldings, mantels, and built-in bookcases.

Naturally, once you decide upon a color scheme, you'll want to achieve pleasing, long-lasting results. In regard to paint, satin finishes (having a slight sheen) are ideal for living rooms, bedrooms, and dining rooms, where

occasional wiping with a damp sponge may be required. For hard-working rooms, such as the kitchen and bath, and for woodwork that tends to accumulate fingerprints, a semigloss paint will facilitate cleaning. Flat paints can be used on ceilings and in low traffic areas where smudges are unlikely.

The chapters that follow examine specific natural color palettes and present a plethora of inspiring ideas for bringing the colors you love to the rooms you live in. Never underestimate the power of natural colors—they can transform an ordinary home into the most extraordinary and inviting of settings.

Soft Neutrals

Several of the beautiful colors found in nature are what we refer to as neutral hues. Variations of cream, beige, sand, and taupe, as well as the numerous whites, allow for versatile, timeless, and soothing interiors. And let's not forget gray, which can present a calming, subtle backdrop. These natural colors have the powerful ability to recall such scenes as a sparkling, crisp winter day, a striking desert landscape, or a peaceful ocean beach, where light dances and plays with the hues of smooth pebbles and sandy stretches.

Neutral colors have been used in various dwellings for ages. White, which has long been associated with cleanliness, was symbolic of a joyful home in ancient times. Gray, meanwhile, has historically been linked to spirituality and religious ceremonies. The various shades and tints of brown impart elegance, old-world charm, and even a simple rusticity.

While neutrals can certainly stand alone, they also boast the ability to live harmoniously with stronger colors. Highly versatile, neutral hues work well with contemporary and traditional decors. They often provide the backdrop in Scandinavian country–style rooms and lend an air of sophistication to interiors decorated in American country style.

Neutral colors are frequently chosen for monochromatic schemes that incorporate various tints and shades of a single hue. When a monochromatic or related color scheme is used in a setting, texture becomes an important means of maintaining visual interest. For example, wood flooring, lace curtains, wicker furniture, and such accessories as baskets and flowers can all bear similar hues, yet at the same time provide a sense of variety that will enhance the decorative picture. Architectural details, such as moldings, can also pitch in to add another dimension.

Opposite: Taupe walls are accompanied by accents of white—in the architectural trim, built-in bookcases, and wood-beamed vaulted ceiling—to help keep this subdued setting uplifting. Airy curtains that admit plenty of natural light also help to brighten up the space. By leaving the hardwood floor bare, the owner has achieved a refined yet natural look that warms up the room.

Neutral colors can, of course, team up with bolder shades, and there are certain pairings that work particularly well. White, of course, goes with everything, whether it makes up the backdrop or manifests itself as the predominant color. Cream works quite nicely with greens and blues, while gray makes a handsome companion for pink. And sand and beige are flattered by black, dark blue, or a softer pale blue.

Obviously, your walls offer the largest canvases when it comes to color. Paint is the most cost-effective and flexible choice for a wall treatment, and there are even textured paints that provide an extra dimension. However, you are by no means restricted to paint; myriad options await beyond this realm. A monochromatic wallpaper with a subtle design (stripes perhaps), beadboard wainscoting painted a soft white, and pale wood paneling are but a few of the possibilities for heightening a room's charisma. When mulling over your options, think about the mood that each wall treatment evokes. Does something with a casual feel or a more formal air best suit your style?

When it comes to flooring, neutral colors are naturals. Hardwood, plank, painted, and parquet flooring all lend themselves to a neutral color scheme. In addition, carpeting—especially something with a notable texture such as a Berber rug—will help keep the decor engaging. Stone flooring can introduce such hues as pale gray, beige, or buff, while the vast world of tile offers a never-ending array of demeanors and practical benefits. For added comfort and color underfoot, an Oriental area rug can supply a fitting decorative touch. Other welcome coverings include nubby rag rugs and area rugs composed of such natural fibers as sisal, coir, jute, and sea grass. Made from plants grown in South America, Africa, or Asia, natural fiber rugs are available in different sizes and are often accessorized with decorative bindings. Sisal rugs, the most popular of the natural fiber species, are durable and can be dyed different colors. One word of caution, however: natural fiber rugs can be difficult to clean and will show stains. With this in mind, it's probably best to reserve them for select rooms that don't have a lot of traffic or opt for wool carpeting that has the look of sisal.

For window dressings, think airy lace curtains, patterned or textured sheers, wood shutters, fabric blinds, cotton curtains, bamboo shades, or stunning drapes made of silk or brocade. Clear indicators of a relaxed or formal tone, window treatments contribute an abundance of decorative style. For example, lace lends a gentle touch of romance and cottage charm, while a layered treatment speaks of opulence. Fabric shades can go contemporary, while shutters can imbue a room with simple rustic appeal.

Furnishings, which above all should be comfortable, can be accented with strong textures, such as wicker or wood. Depending upon your personal style, your rooms may call for refined pieces or a casual, plump sofa and cozy easy chairs that invite curling up. Upholstery in neutral hues is available in a wide range of materials and patterns. Slipcovers, too, lend easy elegance in a soft white or beige.

Finishing touches include everything from artwork and favorite collections to woven throws and toss pillows to such natural elements as green plants, baskets, and seashells. Also consider adding black accents (in lamp bases or frames), a display of vintage creamware, or glassware in nature-inspired colors. With a neutral palette, it's easy to change your decorative accessories to reflect the change in the seasons—such subtle variations can breathe new life into your favorite rooms on a fairly regular basis.

Last, but certainly not least, neutral colors can be highly successful in the kitchen and bath. Wood cabinetry—especially pale wood tones—and painted-white cabinetry will blend beautifully with modern appliances and fixtures. Consider using such decorative elements as tile in a neutral or bolder shade (for accent) or with a hand-painted design to create a signature touch. Appliances, available in a wide range of colors including white, black, and sand, are a snap to coordinate with a neutral color scheme.

Above: PUNCTUATING A WHITE BACKGROUND WITH OTHER NEUTRAL COLORS ACHIEVES A SUBTLY REFINED LOOK, AS EVIDENCED BY THIS LIVING ROOM. SAND-COLORED CUSHIONS ON THE WINDOW SEAT PROMISE THE PEACEFUL REPOSE OF RELAXING ON THE BEACH. MEANWHILE, BLACK ACCENTS—IN THE CHAIR AND PICTURE FRAMES—ADD A SOPHISTICATED FLAIR. NOTE, TOO, THE BEAUTIFUL, NATURAL TEXTURES OF THE STONE HEARTH AND LUSH GREEN PLANTS.

Right: HERE, NATURAL ELEMENTS MAKE UP A NEUTRAL PALETTE. WALLS OF HORIZONTAL PLANKING AND A TONGUE-AND-GROOVE CEILING, BOTH OF WHICH ARE LEFT UNPAINTED TO LET THEIR NATURAL GRAINING SHINE, GIVE THIS HOME A CASUAL FEEL. THE RUSTIC MOOD IS AUGMENTED BY EARTHY TERRA-COTTA FLOOR TILES, WARM WOODEN FURNISHINGS, AND A NAVAJO RUG. A LARGE SUPPLY OF LOGS, NESTLED SNUGLY INTO THE SIDE OF A STONE FIREPLACE, ENHANCES THE NATURAL LOOK AND PROMISES THAT A COMFORTING FIRE CAN BE HAD AT A MOMENT'S NOTICE.

Above: Various shades of white have been used in tandem to fashion a tranquil and inviting living room.

Though painted in the same hue as the rest of the walls, chair rails pop out to prevent these surfaces from seeming too bland.

Meanwhile, blond wooden furnishings add another touch of variety, yet maintain the creamy look. Plump pillows and potted palms

heighten the alluring nature of this room, where comfort is of the utmost importance.

Above: PALE WOOD TONES GIVE THIS CONTEMPORARY DINING ROOM A CLEAN, STREAMLINED APPEARANCE. IN THE ADJOINING LIVING ROOM, SLIDING GLASS DOORS AND A VAST SKYLIGHT ENHANCE THE REFRESHING LOOK BY USHERING IN SUNLIGHT AND BRINGING NATURE INDOORS. NATURE IS FURTHER INCORPORATED INTO THE DECOR BY THE CHAIR UPHOLSTERY, WHICH FEATURES A SWIRLING VINE DESIGN THAT PICKS UP THE BLOND TONES OF THE TABLE AND FLOOR.

Opposite: A CONTEMPORARY SPACE IS INFUSED WITH ELEGANCE, COURTESY OF LINEN-COLORED WALLS, STRONG TEXTURES, AND PROMINENT ACCENT COLORS. THE FOCAL POINT IS AN ORNAMENTAL SCREEN THAT COMMANDS ATTENTION WITH ITS BOLD PATTERN AND POWERFUL SPLASHES OF BROWN AND BLACK, YET LINKS ITSELF TO THE SETTING BY SPORTING TOUCHES OF THE HUE THAT GRACES THE WALLS. THE COMBINATION OF THE DARK WOOD TABLE AND WHITE UPHOLSTERY PROVIDES SIMILAR CONTRAST.

Above: DRESSED COMPLETELY IN WHITE AND DRAPED WITH A GAUZY CANOPY, THIS BED CREATES THE SENSATION OF FLOATING ON A CLOUD. CHERUBS FLUTTERING ABOVE THE MIRROR ENHANCE THE HEAVENLY FEELING, WHILE NATURAL FIBER RUGS PAIRED WITH A GRAY AND WHITE MARBLE FLOOR CREATE THE ILLUSION OF A STORMY SEA AND PATCHES OF DRY LAND BELOW. THE OVERALL FEELING IS ONE OF COZINESS AND SECURITY.

Left: Taupe and white make a stunning duo in this bedroom retreat. The architectural molding and the beamed ceiling are spotlighted by white paint that provides contrast against the walls. A gray metal cabinet serves as a novel bedside table, while the black bed sports smooth white linens. Providing the perfect finishing touch, a black-and-white photograph of a landscape hangs next to the bed.

Opposite: THANKS TO THE TREATMENT OF THE COFFERED CEILING, THIS KITCHEN IS COMPLETELY ENVELOPED IN A NATURAL COLOR PALETTE. BY PAINTING EACH SECTION A SLIGHTLY DIFFERENT SHADE, THE OWNERS HAVE CREATED A HIGHLY ENGAGING DISPLAY THAT FLOWS DOWN TO THE UPPER PORTION OF THE WALLS. THE DIVIDING WHITE TRIM, WHICH ECHOES THE CABINETRY, CALLS ATTENTION TO THE CEILING, WHILE RECESSED LIGHTING PERFORMS ITS SERVICE WITHOUT DETRACTING FROM THE DESIGN.

Above: THIS STATE-OF-THE-ART KITCHEN FEATURES A NEUTRAL COLOR SCHEME FOR A CLEAN, SMART LOOK. PALE WOOD CABINETRY AND A TILE FLOOR BEARING VARIATIONS OF GRAY AND BEIGE ARE BROUGHT TO LIFE BY THE BLACK COUNTERTOP AND SEATING AT THE ISLAND. TILES THAT ECHO THE HUE OF THE CABINETRY JOIN ONES IN A DEEPER BROWN TO FORM AN EYE-CATCHING BACKSPLASH THAT BECOMES AN INSTANT FOCAL POINT.

Opposite: PALE, CREAMY TILES, A STONE VANITY WITH SUBTLE COLOR VARIATIONS, AND A SIMILARLY HUED STONE BASIN IMBUE THIS BATHROOM WITH THE SERENITY OF A SPA. A GLEAMING METAL-FRAMED MIRROR AND A TRIO OF SILVER BUD VASES ADD A TOUCH OF ELEGANCE TO THE SCENE, WHICH BRINGS TO MIND THE WHITE SANDS OF GREECE.

Above: A WHITE PEDESTAL SINK AND A PALE WOOD VANITY GIVE THIS ROOM A SLIGHTLY SCANDINAVIAN FEEL. BEIGE WALLS AND WHITE TRIM ESTABLISH A QUIET BACKDROP THAT IS WARMED BY TILE FLOORING AND GREENERY. TOGETHER, THESE ELEMENTS CREATE A CASUAL ATMOSPHERE—PERFECT FOR A LONG SOAK IN THE TUB. **Right:** A SIMPLE DECOR CAN INDEED BE QUITE STRIKING WHEN DECKED IN NEUTRAL COLORS. WHITE WALLS AND NATURAL FIBER CARPETING ARE PUNCTUATED BY A BLACK CLAW-FOOT TUB AND DELICATE-LOOKING METAL SHELVING THAT HOLDS A GENEROUS SUPPLY OF PLUSH, WHITE TOWELS. THANKS TO THE CONTINUATION OF THE COLOR SCHEME INTO THE BEDROOM, WHICH IS VISIBLE THROUGH THE ARCH, ONE ROOM FLOWS SMOOTHLY INTO THE NEXT.

Subtle Pastels

Pastels, those soft colors reminiscent of a spring day, can be used to create breathtaking rooms. Especially at home in settings with an abundance of natural light, pastels in either warm or cool hues can metamorphose a small space into one that seems airy and expansive. Pale blue, which has long been associated with happiness, will set a soothing tone, while a soft pink will liven up a bath, especially when combined with shiny white fixtures. A light and creamy yellow, symbolic of intellectual growth, is often favored for kitchens because of its fresh and cheerful demeanor. And apricot, pale peach, or even a mint green can transform a living room into an inviting family retreat. The options are almost limitless.

Pastel colors are created by mixing white with a primary or secondary color; for instance, pink is a mixture of white and red. These hues first became fashionable during the eighteenth century in France, where rococo bedchambers were transformed with soft tints that added a whole new dimension. Pastels have been popular ever since, particularly with those who see nature in these charming hues and long to bring a gentle hint of the outdoors inside. Just savoring the beauty of a flower garden reveals nature-created pastel colors—the pink rose, the pale yellow daffodil, the soft blue of Jacob's ladder. Due to their light tone, pastels have long been considered feminine colors. Pink, often viewed as the most feminine of them all, is symbolic of love and romance, as is its primary component—red.

White trim and accents are ideal for keeping sprightly pastels in line and preventing them from overwhelming a space. Other colors, such as muted shades and jewel tones, also coordinate pleasantly with pastels, creating interesting visual dynamics. A perfect example is a complementary color scheme (one that includes any two opposing colors on the color wheel). Pink can be joined by a deep green, or a pale yellow can be enhanced with a

Opposite: IN THIS LIGHT AND AIRY SETTING, PASTELS ARE INTRODUCED THROUGH A TILED FIREPLACE SURROUND. THE WARM PINK AND APRICOT HUES MATCH THE WARMTH OF THE PINE FLOOR. TOSS PILLOWS IN SIMILAR HUES, WITH SOME BLUE AND GREEN ACCENTS, CONTRIBUTE TO THE OVERALL APPEAL.

royal blue. Neutral colors, especially in the form of rugs or furnishings, can also be blended into a pastel palette with great success.

If you intend to paint walls in a pastel hue, select a paint with a flat or satin finish to avoid creating an intense sheen. By incorporating white trim, you can make architectural elements, such as cornices, picture rails, chair rails, and built-in bookcases, more pronounced. The same effect can be achieved by using a deeper pastel for these details.

When it comes to wallpaper, perpetual favorites are mini prints, stripes, and floral designs; these are generally linked to cottage, country, or Victorian Revival decors. However, pastel wallpapers can be used successfully in contemporary settings, rooms with an Art Deco flair, and Scandinavian interiors, as well.

Flooring options for a pastel color scheme range from hardwoods and planking to carpeting, tile, and decorative rugs. Pastels work wonderfully with the warmer wood tones found in such popular woods as oak and honey pine. Terra-cotta tiles, whose orangy hues cast a soft glow on the surroundings, make an agreeable match for pink or apricot walls. And a faded Oriental rug bearing cool jewel tones will deftly enhance a pale blue or mint green backdrop.

Faded fabrics, as well as ones deliberately "aged" (soaked in tea), often go hand in hand with pastel colors. Florals and stripes are among the obvious choices, but since there are no hard-and-fast rules, select upholstery and drapes that successfully convey your personal style. Plump sofas and easy chairs, wicker painted white, faux-bamboo tables, and rosewood or mahogany furnishings are perfect for a cottage decor, while black accents, cream trim, and chrome tables recall Art Deco styling.

Windows dressed in lace, bamboo shades, chintz curtains, or luxurious silk drapes are but a few possibilities when working with a pastel color scheme. Lace, available in white or "natural," has the advantage of adding both texture and pattern. Plus, its delicate nature makes it a highly suitable mate for flowery hues.

Decorative accessories that work well with pastels include gilt-trimmed frames, floral bouquets, green plants, baskets, jewel-toned pillows, botanical prints, wall-hung tapestries, wall-hung plates with floral motifs, and landscapes and seascapes, to name a few. When pastels are used in a beach home or vacation retreat, blue is generally the color of choice, and shell collections, miniature boats, and striped pillows often chime in.

Kitchens and baths are well suited to nature-inspired pastels. In the kitchen, cabinetry can be painted almost any color from soft blue to pale green or yellow to lighten up the space. And in the bath, white fixtures will gleam against your favorite pastel tint. Color coordinate the appropriate accessories, or add complementary colors for added flair. Towels, for instance, are a wonderfully simple means for introducing an accent color into the bath.

Above: A WHITE SPACE TAKES ON RELAXING AND UNDERSTATED BEAUTY WHEN OUTFITTED IN PALE BLUES. THE UPHOLSTERED HEADBOARD, IN A MEDIUM BLUE,

BECOMES A STRIKING FOCAL POINT, WHILE THE SOFT BLUE AND WHITE FLORAL SPREAD PROVIDES A GRACEFUL TRANSITION TO THE SURROUNDING WHITENESS. MIXING

PATTERNS IS A WONDERFUL WAY OF BLENDING COLORS—AS EVIDENCED BY THE WAY THE BED PRACTICALLY FLOWS INTO THE CHECKERED CHAISE LONGUE.

Right: Pastels mixed with light or bleached woods can run the risk of making a room seem too pale. In this dining room, a soft lavender and white color scheme is indeed blended with light woods, but the pastel hue acts as an accent color (manifesting itself in the chairs and area rug) rather than providing the decorative focus. By introducing a black-and-white photograph and silver objects, the owners have given the space a polished look.

Opposite: Painted pink, the walls in this welcoming living room present a sweet demeanor that's not too syrupy, thanks to the use of white paint on the architectural trim. With pastels, texture becomes an important component of the decor, preventing rooms from appearing too bland. The wicker coffee table and chair, resembling furnishings often found on a porch, bring a taste of the outdoors inside.

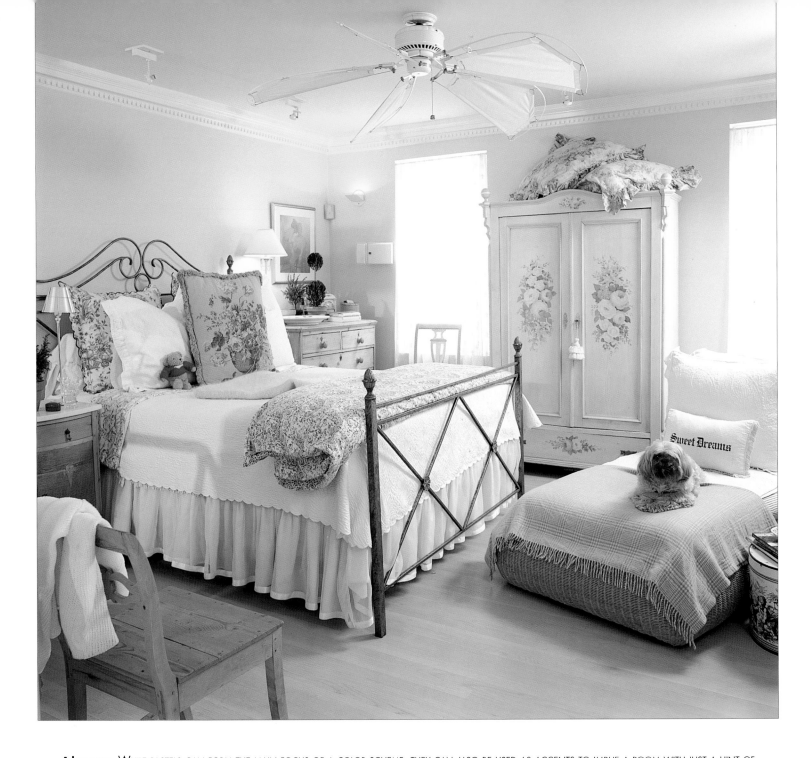

Above: While pastels can form the main focus of a color scheme, they can also be used as accents to imbue a room with just a hint of springtime. This casually elegant bedroom, designed with neutral hues that include gray, white, and tan, also features a striking armoire with hand-painted blooms. On the bed, a needlework pillow bearing flowers repeats the subtle infusion of pinks and purples.

Left: TEXTURED GREEN WALLS TEAM UP WITH A FLORAL-PATTERNED CANOPY TO CREATE THE SENSATION OF SLEEPING IN A MEADOW OF WILDFLOWERS. THE PASTEL TINTS OF THE WALLS AND PILLOWS PROVIDE A SOOTHING COUNTERPOINT TO THE STRONGER HUES OF THE FLORAL DESIGN, WHICH IS REPEATED IN THE BEDSIDE ARMCHAIR. THE RESULTING PICTURE IS A PERFECT EXAMPLE OF HOW PASTELS CAN MIX GRACEFULLY WITH OTHER NATURE-INSPIRED HUES.

Above: A BEAUTIFUL PASTEL BLUE, REMINISCENT OF A CLEAR SKY, COVERS THE CEILING AND MUCH OF THE TRIM IN THIS SPACIOUS KITCHEN—AS WELL AS THE LIVING ROOM BEYOND. WHITE CABINETRY, COUNTERTOPS, AND A WHITE TILE BACKSPLASH MAINTAIN THE AIRY QUALITY OF THE SPACE, WHICH HAS BEEN ESTABLISHED BY AN ABUNDANT USE OF GLASS. NOTE THAT DECORATIVE TOUCHES HAVE BEEN KEPT TO A MINIMUM, ALLOWING THE SCENIC COLOR SCHEME TO BE THE FOCUS OF ATTENTION.

Opposite: IN THIS WELCOMING EAT-IN KITCHEN, A WHITE COUNTERTOP AND TILE BACKSPLASH BREAK UP THE EXPANSE OF MINT GREEN WALLS. THE COOL COLOR SCHEME IS WARMED BY A WOODEN HARVEST TABLE AND SIDE TABLE, AS WELL AS SUCH NATURAL ACCENTS AS A BOWL OF ORANGES, A BASKET OF GOURDS, AND A PLANT ARRANGEMENT. BENCHES AT THE TABLE COMBINE WITH THE GREEN BACKGROUND TO CREATE A PICNICLIKE ATMOSPHERE.

Left: APRICOT WALLS ARE A SMART CHOICE FOR A SMALL KITCHEN, SINCE THIS SOFT TINT NOT ONLY MAKES A ROOM APPEAR LARGER, BUT ALSO MAINTAINS THE WARMTH OF A COZY SPACE. HERE, THE APRICOT HUE POPS UP AGAIN IN THE TILE COUNTERTOP, WHILE PALE YELLOW CABINETS PROVIDE A MELODIOUS INTERLUDE. GLEAMING COPPER COOKWARE IS SHOWN OFF TO ADVANTAGE BY THE WALL COLOR, WHILE A LIGHT GREEN VINTAGE STOVE ADDS APPEALING CONTRAST.

Left: PASTELS ARE OFTEN ASSOCIATED WITH COTTAGE DECOR, BUT HERE'S PROOF POSITIVE THAT THEY ARE HIGHLY VERSATILE. IN THIS CONTEMPORARY LIVING ROOM, PALE GREEN WALLS, NEUTRAL CARPETING, AND WHITE SLIPCOVERS ESTABLISH A SERENE TONE THAT HELPS PUT FAMILY MEMBERS AND GUESTS AT EASE. THANKS TO THE SOFT BACKDROP, THE ARTISTIC TABLES, WITH THEIR DEEPER HUES, ARE ALLOWED TO TAKE CENTER STAGE.

Above: WOODEN WAINSCOTING HAS BEEN PAINTED A PASTEL YELLOW TO BRING A TOUCH OF SUNSHINE TO A FORMERLY DARK HALLWAY. THE WHITE BASEBOARD AND UPPER PORTION OF THE WALL HELP TO LIGHTEN THE SPACE FURTHER. THE HORIZONTAL STENCILED BORDER SPORTS YELLOW DIAMONDS THAT LINK IT TO THE WAINSCOTING, WHILE THE MOSS-COLORED MOLDING ECHOES THE COLOR OF THE PAINTED TABLE.

Right: HERE, A MONOCHRO-
MATIC PALETTE CALLS UPON VARIOUS
TONES OF YELLOW TO CREATE A
SUMMERY BATH. DEEP SHADES OF
YELLOW IN THE WINDOW DRESSING
ARE JOINED BY A PALE YELLOW
GRACING THE VANITY AND SHELVES
TO FORM A CREAMY BLEND. WHITE
PULLS, WHITE FLOWERS, AND A
PRIMARILY WHITE MARBLE COUNTER
PROVIDE VARIETY AND GIVE THE
SPACE A PRIM LOOK.

CALMING BLUES AND FOREST GREENS

Ask several people what their favorite color is and, undoubtedly, the majority will say blue. It's no wonder— blue promotes a sense of well-being and tranquility. The color of the sky and the sea, it has long been associated with spirituality, royalty, and justice. Its many variations blend splendidly with numerous other colors, and its coolness establishes a peaceful tone when used in the home. While blue is often preferred for bedrooms, thanks to its restful nature, it has also been used for centuries in kitchens throughout Europe, where it is linked to cleanliness and celebrated in the renowned designs of Delft tiles.

Blue and white is a popular combination for both traditional and country decors, but the possibilities don't stop there. Blues can be mixed with greens or yellows, as well as with rich jewel tones, such as gold, burgundy, or crimson, for an elegant look. Highly versatile, blue also provides an attractive, solid splash of color in contemporary settings decked out in grays and other neutral tones. When decorating a room, consider the darker shades, such as navy, sapphire, and cobalt, as well as the mid-range hues, which include sky blue, iris, cornflower blue, turquoise, and French blue. These are but a small sampling of the myriad blues that will evoke the spirit of the outdoors when showcased inside.

Green brings to mind forests and fields, as well as the fruits, vegetables, and flowers that grow within these natural settings. There seems to be no end to the greens found in the countryside, and several of these enchanting hues can be used to create refreshing environments throughout the home. Appropriately, green is symbolic of life and fertility; we have only to look out the window on a spring day and witness the budding green leaves to be reminded of the incredible vitality associated with this color.

Certain greens can be used to create stately backgrounds indoors. For instance, forest green achieves a sedate and refined tone in a library, while a medium green may be just the color to outfit your garden room. Possessing a deeper tone than the pastel tints, such mid-range greens

Opposite: A FOUR-POSTER BED COMMANDS ATTENTION IN THIS SUBDUED SETTING. THE WALLS ARE PAINTED A SEDATE GREEN WITH DELICATE WHITE VEINING THAT HINTS AT TREE BRANCHES AND LEAVES. A WHITE CEILING AND WHITE ACCENTS LEND AN AIRY QUALITY WHILE MAINTAINING THE TRANQUIL TONE. LEAFY PLANTS ARE SIMPLE TOUCHES THAT COMPLETE THE PICTURE OF A FOREST GLEN.

as moss, olive, and sage can be combined with white or cream to form an elegant backdrop. Depending upon the particular shade of green you select, you can add other greens of a similar tone, touches of blue, neutral colors, yellow, pink, or gold.

Both blue and green have played large roles in the history of interior design throughout Europe, so it's no wonder that either color can serve as the starting point for an English country, Scandinavian, Mediterranean, or French country decor. In the annals of North American design, blue has always held a prominent place, while green became fashionable in Victorian and Arts and Crafts decors. Since rigid limits are no longer imposed upon color when it comes to home decorating, blue and/or green can be used with any of the styles mentioned above, as well as for more modern interiors.

As with any color, paint is an excellent means for establishing a blue or green background, but wallpaper may be called upon for texture and panache. Many of the striking Arts and Crafts wallpaper designs made popular by William Morris (and being reproduced today) incorporate beautiful muted shades of blue and green. There are also numerous striped, floral, and geometric patterns to select from, as well as French toile de Jouy wallpapers, which blend quite pleasantly and harmoniously with checked and floral fabrics.

Since deep and medium shades of blue and green have a strength about them, they call for flooring that holds its own. Oak and parquet floors, richly toned wall-to-wall carpeting, and jewel-colored Oriental rugs certainly will not fade into the background, and they work well in living rooms, dining rooms, or bedrooms. Ceramic tile, as well as resilient flooring in one of the many colors and patterns available today, is highly suitable for the kitchen and bath. And speaking of tile, consider the possibilities for designing a decorative backsplash or countertop in the kitchen. Hand-painted tiles will not only provide additional dashes of color, but will also bring an original touch to the setting.

Since medium- or deep-shaded cool colors can establish a peaceful mood, they are often the ideal candidates for a sumptuous window dressing. Rich draperies made of damask, velvet, or a toile de Jouy will imbue a room with semiformal or formal airs, while a crisp gingham or Provençal fabric creates an easygoing feel. Other options include Roman shades, which can be custom-made to match upholstery for a coordinated look, or wooden shutters coated with a dark stain or a white painted finish for a streamlined treatment that has a hint of architectural flair.

Nature-inspired blues and greens can also be introduced into a living room, bedroom, or dining room via furnishings upholstered in these color categories. Stripes, checks, chintz, and other florals can work well, but don't overlook other options, such as a striking paisley or a tartan plaid, both of which can be lovely in a family room or library. Keep in mind, mixing different patterns in a single

Left: Is it a bedroom or a garden retreat? With its refreshing apple green walls, this cheerful bedroom makes it easier to rise and shine in the morning. Sunny yellow curtains with a leafy design enhance the summery look, regardless of the time of year. While red tulips currently provide an additional dash of color, these can be replaced by other flowers for a slight change of scenery.

room is an effective way of adding visual drama when the color scheme focuses on a single hue. Other furnishings that blend beautifully with blues and greens include darker wood pieces, faux bamboo, metals (with a silver finish), and painted pieces. Picture an indigo blue step-back cupboard in the eat-in kitchen, hunter green bookcases in the study, or Shaker cabinets, wearing their signature gray-blue, in the dining area. In garden rooms, metal and wicker furnishings are often painted green to link the space to the outdoors.

There is a glorious assortment of decorative accessories that can be called upon to give a home distinct touches of blue or green. Rustic pottery, for example, has a certain old-world charm, while glassware sparkles in colors ranging from sea blue to bottle green. Blue and white china is an obvious choice, and a display of willow pattern dishes can be arranged in a glass-front cabinet or situated gallery-style on a prominent wall. Pewter and silver candlesticks make fitting accessories when blues or greens sport a little gray. Even the bath can be dressed to the nines when luxurious towels and fresh flowers are chosen to flatter a blue or green theme. Remember, too, you can change accessories to reflect the seasons, your mood, or the intended purpose of a room.

Above: TIMELESS ELEGANCE IS CONVEYED IN A LIVING ROOM WHERE FURNISHINGS AND WINDOWS ARE DRESSED IN GREEN. WHITE WALLS AND BEIGE CARPETING PROVIDE A QUIET BACKGROUND FOR A FOREST GREEN SOFA AND A TOILE-COVERED EASY CHAIR WITH A DARK GREEN WOODLAND PATTERN. THIS SAME FABRIC IS USED FOR THE WINDOW SHADES TO GIVE THE ROOM A COORDINATED LOOK. THE CHECKERED WING CHAIR, THE MINI PRINT ON THE OTTOMAN, AND THE FLORAL DESIGN ON THE TOSS PILLOW BRIGHTEN THE SCENE, JUST LIKE COLORFUL BLOOMS DOTTING A WILDERNESS SETTING.

Above: SINCE GREEN IS A MIND-SOOTHING COLOR, IT'S THE PERFECT CHOICE FOR A HOME LIBRARY. HUNTER GREEN BOOKSHELVES, WALLS, AND

MULLIONS GIVE A RESTFUL QUALITY TO THIS ROOM DEVOTED TO QUIET PURSUITS. IN ORDER TO TEMPER THE DARKER TONES, THE OWNERS HAVE

INCORPORATED FLORAL CURTAINS, A NATURAL FIBER RUG, AND CHUNKY BASKETS.

Opposite: BATHED IN BLUE, THIS DINING ROOM CEILING APPEARS TO BRING THE SKY INDOORS. WHITE WALLS ARE ACCENTED WITH THE SAME SHADE OF BLUE ON THE DOOR AND WINDOW FRAMES, ACTING AS A FOIL FOR THE DARK WOOD FURNISHINGS AND HANDSOME WOOD FLOOR. **Right:** SUBTLE INFUSIONS OF BLUE CREATE A PEACEFUL RETREAT IN THIS CHARMING BEDROOM. ON THE CEILING, A PAINTED SKY, COMPLETE WITH SWIRLS OF CLOUDS, CREATES THE FEELING OF SLEEPING OUTDOORS—A SENSATION THAT IS ENHANCED BY THE RUSTIC TWIG FURNISHINGS. INDEED, WITH ITS CANOPIED STYLING, THE BED RESEMBLES A SHELTERING NATURAL BOWER THAT IS SURE TO LULL OCCUPANTS INTO A SOUND SLEEP. ACCENTS OF BLUE, SEEN IN THE BLANKET AND SOFA PILLOWS, ARE SPRINKLED ACROSS THE ROOM TO TIE THE SPACE TOGETHER.

Above: THANKS TO A STUNNING PAINT TREATMENT, THESE AQUAMARINE WALLS RESEMBLE A MEDITERRANEAN SEASCAPE, WITH WISPS OF WHITE REMINISCENT OF

WHITECAPS. THE COOL AND SERENE CANVAS IS WARMED BY PLANK FLOORING, SIMILAR TO THAT OF A YACHT, AND A SHELL-FRAMED MIRROR THAT CARRIES OUT THE BEACH

THEME. THE PREDOMINANT BLUE AND WHITE COLOR SCHEME IS EXTENDED BY THE BEDSPREAD, SHEER CURTAINS, VELVET UPHOLSTERY, AND ARCHITECTURAL DETAILS.

Above: In this spare but attractive bathroom, a beamed ceiling and a reddish floor are complemented by various shades of blue, which pop up on the walls, tub surround, cupboard, and window frame. The blues enhance the minimalist decor while maintaining the rustic look of the space.

Above: JUST THE RIGHT AMOUNT OF DARK GREEN HAS BEEN INTRODUCED INTO THIS SPACIOUS KITCHEN—ENOUGH TO ADD DRAMA BUT NOT OVERWHELM. THE TEXTURED WALL TREATMENT HEIGHTENS THE NATURAL LOOK, CREATING A MOSSY FINISH. BY TEMPERING THE WALLS WITH A WHITE WOOD-BEAMED CEILING, WHITE CABINETRY, AN EARTHY TILE FLOOR, AND WOOD COUNTERTOPS, THE OWNERS HAVE ESTABLISHED A REASSURING SENSE OF BALANCE. SKYLIGHTS IN THE VAULTED CEILING PROVIDE ADDITIONAL NATURAL LIGHTING SO WALLS DON'T APPEAR TOO DARK. NOTE HOW THE COLOR-COORDINATED LIGHTING FIXTURES ENHANCE THE PALETTE.

Right: Custom-crafted cabinets, which look more like elegant furnishings, display a moss green trim that reinforces the green tile backsplash and window surround. Tile is an effective means for introducing both color and texture into the kitchen. In this particular case, the various green hues at the window seem to bridge the gap between the interior and the natural beauty beyond the panes.

Left: Royal blue walls with white trim give this dining room a majestic look. With their formal airs, gilt frames, a staggered display of blue and white china, and regal tassels on the dining room chairs contribute to the sumptuous look. Visual drama is introduced by the red in the cushions, as well as the rich red paint on the walls of the adjoining room.

Above: HUNTER GREEN ACCENTS PUNCTUATE A CONTEMPORARY KITCHEN DESIGNED WITH NEUTRAL HUES AND PASTEL GREEN WALLS. BY INTRODUCING A WOODLAND COLOR, THE OWNERS HAVE LINKED THE SPACE TO THE TREES OUTSIDE, SEEN THROUGH THE GLASS-FITTED DOOR. FOR ADDED MEASURE, A FLORAL ARRANGEMENT BOASTING LUSH GREEN LEAVES HAS BEEN PLACED ON THE COUNTER. **Right:** A FRENCH COUNTRY KITCHEN IS COLOR-WASHED WITH DELPHINIUM BLUE. THANKS TO A SOFTENING PAINT TECHNIQUE, THIS STRONG BLUE IS NOT OVERPOWERING. A GENEROUS BANK OF WINDOWS, WHICH AFFORDS PLENTY OF NATURAL LIGHT, ALSO HELPS PREVENT THE SPACE FROM SEEMING TOO INTENSE. GOLDEN WOOD TONES, KITCHEN-WARE ON DISPLAY, AND NATURAL GREENERY GIVE THE ROOM TEXTURE, WHILE A BRIGHT WHITE STOVE, WHICH CAN CLEARLY HOLD ITS OWN AGAINST THE VIVID BACKDROP, CONTRIBUTES CONTRAST.

Left: CORNFLOWER BLUE WALLS HAVE TRANSFORMED THIS BEDROOM INTO A RESTFUL HAVEN. THE COOL BLUE IS ACCENTUATED BY THE USE OF CRISP WHITE ON THE PAINTED FLOOR, MANTEL, CORNICE, AND CEILING. DEEPER BLUES, ALONG WITH HEARTY RED ACCENTS, ARE FEATURED IN THE AREA RUG AND PATCHWORK QUILT, SUPPLYING A GROUNDING SENSE OF DEPTH. A GILT MIRROR AND AN OAK ARMOIRE PITCH IN TO GIVE THE ROOM ADDITIONAL WARMTH.

Opposite: CLASSIC STYLE IS CLEARLY EVIDENT IN THIS SHAKER-INSPIRED BATH. A DEEP GRAY-GREEN PAINT HAS BEEN USED THROUGH-OUT, APPEARING EVEN ON THE SHAKER PEG RACK. COMBINING THIS SEDATE HUE WITH WHITE ACCENTS NOT ONLY ADHERES TO THE LETTER OF SHAKER STYLE, BUT ALSO MAKES THE SPACE MORE INVITING.

Muted Earth Shades and Harvest Colors

There is perhaps nothing more invigorating than a crisp autumn morning. Autumn is the time of year for strolling the aisles of a lively harvest festival, tending the late blooms in the garden, and simply pausing for a moment here and there to take in the colorful view. Goldenrod, burnt umber, ocher, mocha, crimson, russet, pumpkin, terra-cotta, brick, pale gold—these are the colors of changing leaves, late harvests and flowers, pungent spices, and sun-baked earth.

Earth shades and harvest colors are warm hues that bear a subtle tone. Unlike a vibrant red or bright yellow, these colors have an almost aged or muted look that makes them ideal for interior use. Such browns, reds, and yellows can be called upon to fashion cozy country rooms,

rustic retreats, or elegant surroundings. Their versatility makes them popular choices for understated and timeless designs on everything from wallpaper and upholstery to bedding and dishware.

Muted earth shades and harvest colors can be mixed with one another or with any number of other colors. White or cream can be used in tandem with these earthy hues to give a room a fresh look. Browns, such as burnt umber and a lighter mocha, can be mixed with brick red, blue, or white, while such yellows as ocher and golden-rod pair up nicely with dark reds or deep blues. In the red category, terra-cotta is set off by adding touches of yellow, blue, or medium green. When paired with gold accents, terra-cotta exudes an especially warm, rich look.

Opposite: Rugged natural texture can be a strong purveyor of earthy color. Here, a stone fireplace provides a powerful focal point with its medley of brown hues. Additional browns are brought into the mix by the tone-on-tone sofa and unpainted woodwork, while toss pillows supply refreshing dashes of gold and red. Cream-colored walls serve as a welcome counterpoint to the heavier hues of the space.

Left: EARTHY COLORS AND A
DECORATIVE PAINTING TECHNIQUE
RESULT IN AN ENTRYWAY WITH
EUROPEAN CHARM. A WARM BURNT
SIENNA HAS BEEN CHOSEN FOR
THE WALLS, WHILE A LIGHTER RAW
SIENNA, FEATURING SOFT BROWN
AND PINK TONES, GRACES THE
CEILING, MAKING THE SPACE SEEM
LARGER. BOTH SURFACES HAVE BEEN
SPONGE-PAINTED TO CREATE THE
ILLUSION OF TEXTURE; MEANWHILE,
AN ORIENTAL RUG AND PLUMP
CUSHIONS SUPPLY THE REAL THING.

Earthy hues become all the more beautiful on walls that are color-washed or sponged for a decorative or aged effect. Throughout Italy and France, where such colors predominate, old plaster walls painted in earth shades wear a patina, acquired over time, that reflects the rural countryside. Happily, these same results can be achieved today with patience, time, and minimal skill. How-to books on painting techniques offer step-by-step instructions for achieving the look you desire.

Walls can also be stenciled or dressed with decorative white moldings to set off a palette composed of earth shades. Add a wood-beamed ceiling, and the room is imbued with rustic charm. Of course, if you are fortunate enough to have a brick or stone wall in your home, you can build from this. Wallpapers, too, can be selected in these nature-inspired hues to set a backdrop that works with your particular decorative style.

Possibilities for floors include unglazed terra-cotta tiles, flagstone, pine planking, resilient flooring with a brick pattern, neutral-colored carpeting, and natural fiber rugs. Earthy textures look especially at home with these close-to-the-earth colors and are naturals for a country decor. For a more sophisticated look, carpeting or wood flooring can be layered with Oriental rugs.

Window treatments, depending upon your personal taste and the type of room they will be used in, range from no window dressing at all (to let the view shine) to bamboo shades, matchstick blinds, or heavy drapes.

Shutters, painted white or bearing a light wood stain, can be used to filter light, offer a measure of privacy, and provide substance.

In the living room, dining room, and family room, wood furnishings can be light or dark depending on how casual the room is. Lighter wood tones blended with earth shades and harvest colors are typical of a European country style, while darker woods have a more formal, opulent look and are especially well suited to a traditional decor. Leather sofas and chairs, rush-seat chairs, and bamboo or painted furnishings are a few appropriate options, as are upholstered pieces featuring the colors included in this chapter. Antiques are especially beautiful when showcased against a backdrop of heartening autumnal hues. In bedrooms, you may opt for white furniture and/or bedding to provide contrast against an earthy background.

Kitchens and bathrooms can be stunning when treated to a muted earth shade. Oak cabinetry or cupboards painted white will move your color choice center stage and give the setting a warm, inviting air.

Flattering decorative or finishing touches might include pottery or stoneware, gilt mirrors and picture frames, throw pillows with tassels or fringe, warm throws in neutral hues or earth shades, leather-bound books, baskets for their natural texture, flowers and plants, and brass candlesticks. Don't underestimate the power of accessories, which should be chosen to complement the look and tone of the space.

Right: THIS CONTEMPORARY LIVING ROOM USES A VARIETY OF HARVEST COLORS TO PROVIDE A WARM BACKDROP FOR FURNISHINGS DECKED OUT IN PALE NEUTRAL HUES. A PAIR OF GARNET RED PILLOWS IS ALL IT TAKES TO LINK THE SOFA WITH THE LARGE PIECE OF ART IN THE BACKGROUND. SO THAT THE CONTRAST BETWEEN THE DEEP RED AND LIGHT BEIGE ON THE SOFA IS NOT TOO STARK, A MUTED BLUE-GRAY PILLOW FILLS IN THE GAP AND EASES THE TRANSITION.

Left: THE RICH BROWNS IN THIS SUMPTUOUS LIVING ROOM ARE REMINISCENT OF EXOTIC SPICES OR AUTUMN LEAVES. OCHER WALLS AND CREAMY CARPETING SET THE STAGE FOR THE ARRAY OF BROWN TONES PRESENTED BY THE MOCHA DRAPES AND WINDOW SHADE, THE UPHOLSTERED CHAIRS, AND THE FAWN-COLORED SOFA. LUXURIOUS FABRICS, SUCH AS VELVET OR SATIN, WORK ESPECIALLY WELL WITH A STRONG COLOR, AS THEY TEND TO BRING OUT THE HUE'S LUSTER.

Below: A LUMINOUS GOLDEN BACKDROP DRESSES UP THIS COUNTRY INTERIOR WITH A SLIGHTLY FORMAL AIR, WHICH IS ENHANCED BY THE RICH RED AND GOLD VALANCE. THE PAINTING TECHNIQUE USED TO AGE THE WALLS GIVES THE ROOM A SENSE OF HISTORY.

Opposite: DRAMATIC IMPACT IS THE RESULT WHEN WALLS ARE PAINTED A SATURATED MARIGOLD HUE. BACKING UP A DEEP GREEN FIREPLACE, THE INTENSE COLOR JAZZES UP THE SETTING AND ENERGIZES THE SPACE.

Above: SALMON-COLORED WALLS IMBUE THIS LIVING ROOM WITH ELEGANCE. THE COLOR BLENDS EFFORTLESSLY WITH THE WARM REDS, GOLDS, AND BROWNS, WHICH POP UP IN THE TABLE SKIRT, LAMP, AND TOSS PILLOWS. VELVETY MOSS GREEN UPHOLSTERY ENTICES VISITORS TO MAKE THEMSELVES COMFORTABLE ON THE SETTEE AND PROVIDES GROUNDING CONTRAST. AGAINST THE ORANGISH TONES OF THE BACKDROP, GILT FRAMES ACQUIRE A RICH LOOK.

Opposite: WITH THE HELP OF SOFT LIGHTING, RICH BROWN WALLS BEARING HINTS OF ORANGE CAST A BEAUTIFUL GLOW, IMBUING THIS DINING ROOM WITH A FEELING OF INTIMACY. COLOR CONTINUITY IS ACHIEVED IN THE DINING AREA AND ADJOINING LIVING ROOM WITH THE HELP OF RUGS THAT FEATURE STRONG BLUES. **Right:** A PALE SHADE OF TERRA-COTTA ADDS GENTLE COLOR TO THIS STATELY SETTING. RECALLING THE SIMPLE BEAUTY OF SUN-BAKED CLAY POTS, THIS HUE IS EASY TO LIVE WITH AND MADE ALL THE MORE BEAUTIFUL WHEN BLENDED WITH DARK WOOD TONES. NOTICE HOW THE USE OF OPEN SHELVING ALLOWS THE EARTHY HUE TO SHINE THROUGH, HEIGHTENING THE APPEAL OF THE CHINA DISPLAY. THE BLUE AND WHITE COMBINATION IS REPEATED IN THE AREA RUG, OFFERING SUBTLE CONTRAST AT DIFFERENT LEVELS.

Above: CALLING UPON THE COLORS OF AUTUMN LEAVES, THIS SPACIOUS BEDROOM PRESENTS A BREATHTAKING BLEND OF REDS, ORANGES, YELLOWS, AND BROWNS.

THE USE OF SIMILAR TONES HEIGHTENS THE HARMONY OF THE SCENE, AND THE WARMTH OF THE COLORS MAKES THE LARGE ROOM SEEM COZY.

Right: DRAMATIC WHEN
USED ON A LARGE SCALE, BROWN
TENDS TO HAVE MASCULINE OVER-
TONES. THIS QUALITY IS TEMPERED
HERE BY SOFT TOUCHES, SUCH AS
THE PURPLE AND WINE-COLORED
CANOPY ABOVE THE BED AND THE
PATTERNED THROW.

Opposite: COLOR CONTINUITY IS AN EFFECTIVE STRATEGY WHEN ROOMS ARE ON DISPLAY FROM OTHER AREAS OF THE HOME. HERE, THE DINING ROOM AND KITCHEN ARE CONNECTED BY THE COMPATIBLE HUES OF THEIR WALLS—SCARLET IN THE FORMER, AND A GOLDEN BROWN IN THE LATTER. NOTICE HOW THE SPONGING TECHNIQUE USED ON THE KITCHEN WALLS CREATES A SUBTLE MIX OF TONES, RESULTING IN A TEXTURED APPEARANCE. ARCHITECTURAL FEATURES IN BOTH ROOMS ARE HIGHLIGHTED IN WHITE. **Right:** MUTED TERRA-COTTA TILES FORM A NATURAL-LOOKING BACKSPLASH AND COUNTERTOP IN THIS PROVINCIAL KITCHEN. A BRASS FAUCET MAINTAINS THE WARM LOOK, WHILE THE PATTERNED WALLPAPER TRIM ON THE WINDOW LEDGE LIGHTENS UP THE SCENE A LITTLE WITH ITS SUBDUED PALE GOLDEN HUE. FOR LOVELY COLOR CONTRAST, BLUE CERAMIC POTS PLANTED WITH FLOWERS LINE UP ON THE SILL.

Left: TILE IS A DECORATOR'S DREAM WHEN IT COMES TO GIVING A KITCHEN A DOSE OF COLOR AND PERSONALITY. HERE, THE BACKSPLASH IS PRIMARILY COMPOSED OF EARTH-COLORED TILES, LIGHT AND DARK, WHICH LINK IT TO THE SURROUNDING WOODEN ELEMENTS. SAPPHIRE BLUE TILES POP UP THROUGHOUT THE MIX TO PROVIDE CONTRAST AND TO HELP DRAW THE EYE. UNDER-THE-CABINET FIXTURES NOT ONLY OFFER GREAT TASK LIGHTING, BUT ALSO PLAY UP THE VARIATIONS IN COLOR.

Left: CREAMY FLOORING, WHITE TRIM, A WHITE PEDESTAL SINK, AND A WHITE WINDOW DRESSING PLAY UP WARM OCHER WALLS. A BLACK METAL TOWEL STAND AND A CLASSIC CHAIR WITH BLUE UPHOLSTERY ADD COLOR CONTRAST. ELEGANT TOUCHES, INCLUDING TASSELS AND A GILT MIRROR, IMBUE THE BATH WITH TIMELESS STYLE.

Left: A HARMONIOUS INTERPLAY OF DIFFERENT BROWNS, TEXTURES, AND MATERIALS CONTRIBUTES TO THE RICHNESS OF THIS BATHROOM. NOTICE HOW THE GRAINING OF THE WOOD AND THE SWIRLS AND FLECKS OF THE MARBLE PROVIDE NATURAL DECORATION.

INDEX

PHOTOGRAPHY CREDITS